Globalization
Cooperation and Conflict

by Lisa Benjamin

Table of Contents

Develop Language 2

CHAPTER 1 A World of Cultures 4
Your Turn: Interpret Data 9

CHAPTER 2 Opportunities and Challenges 10
Your Turn: Analyze Cause
and Effect 15

CHAPTER 3 Working Together 16
Your Turn: Read Maps 19

Career Explorations 20
Use Language to Persuade 21
Social Studies Around You 22
Key Words 23
Index 24

DEVELOP LANGUAGE

Many children in the world live in **poverty**. They may not have enough food or a safe place to live. They may not be able to go to school. They may not have good medical care.

Some international organizations work to help these children and their families. Discuss the photos with questions like these.

How are people trying to help children?

Why is education important?

Why is health care important?

What can you do to help children around the world?

poverty – the state of being poor

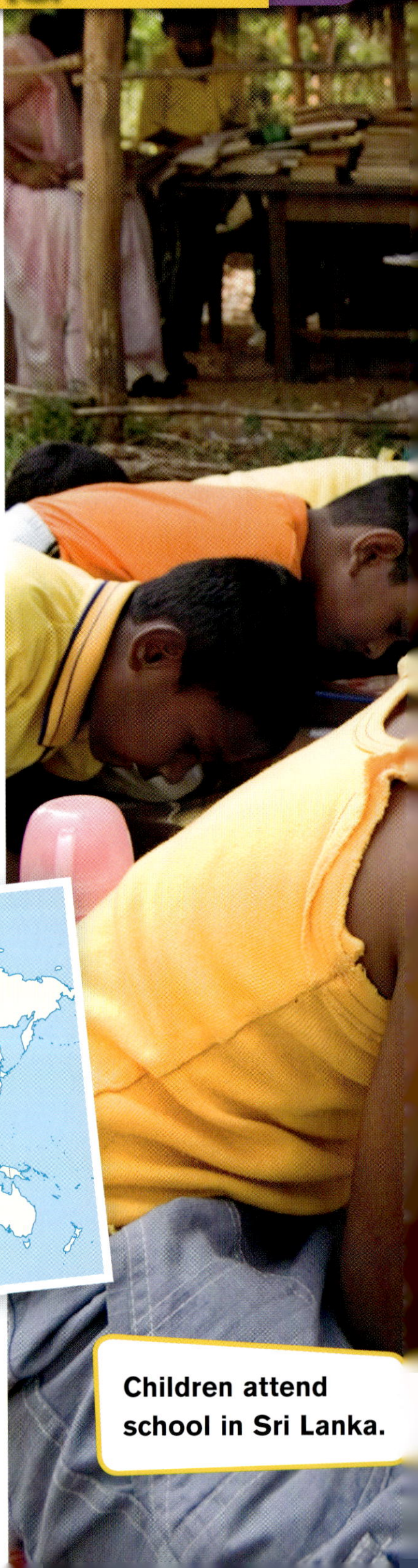

Children attend school in Sri Lanka.

2 *Globalization: Cooperation and Conflict*

Aid workers give food to children in Pakistan.

A doctor treats a child in Darfur, Sudan.

Develop Language

CHAPTER 1

A World of Cultures

In 1271, an explorer named Marco Polo left his home in what is now Italy. For the next three years, he traveled east with his father and his uncle. The three men reached China after a journey of about 5,600 miles. They stayed in Asia for about twenty years.

After Marco Polo returned home in 1295, he wrote a book about his experiences. People in Europe were fascinated by his stories. At that time, wonderful silk, jewels, and spices were sent to Europe from China and India. But almost no one from Europe had traveled all the way to China. People knew very little about China.

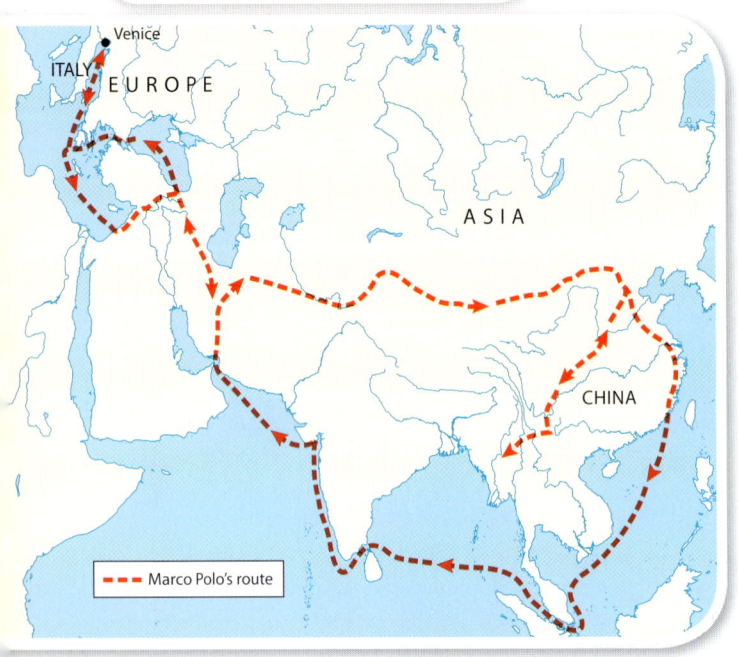

Marco Polo's Travels

Marco Polo traveled by land and sea. He visited many places during his long journey.

4 *Globalization: Cooperation and Conflict*

Marco Polo's book introduced new ideas to people in Europe. For example, people in Europe used gold and silver coins as money. In China, the emperor collected gold, silver, and jewels from people. In return, he gave them paper money. People used paper money throughout China. Marco Polo introduced the idea of paper money to Europe.

Marco Polo lived among people of many different **cultures** during his travels. His travels led to an exchange of cultures and ideas between Europe and Asia.

cultures – ways of life for different groups of people, including their beliefs, customs, art, and behaviors

paper money printed in China in 1274

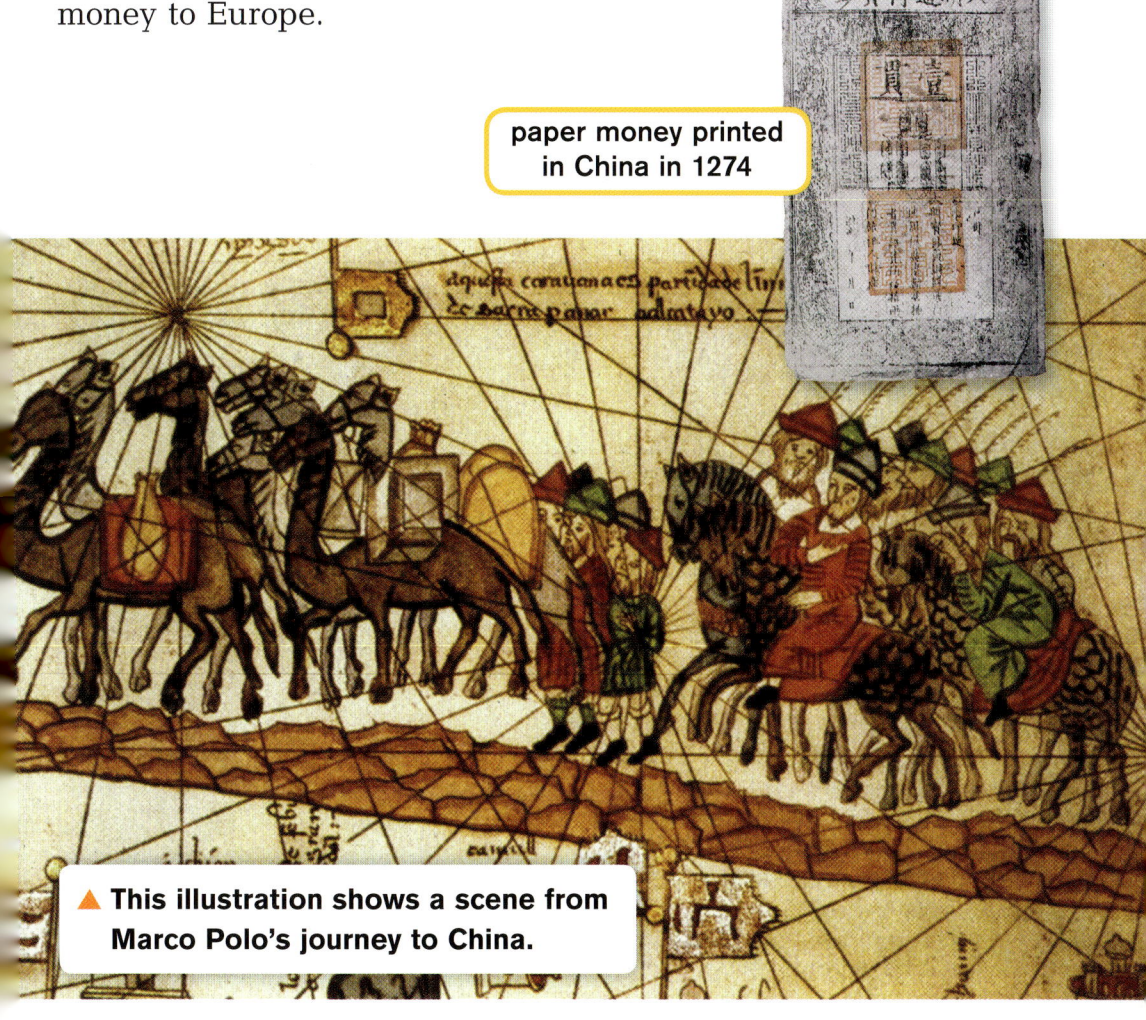

▲ **This illustration shows a scene from Marco Polo's journey to China.**

Chapter 1: A World of Cultures   5

Interacting with Other Cultures

Today, people have many ways to interact with other cultures. People buy **goods** from other countries. Tourists learn about other cultures when they travel.

▲ Restaurants are one way that immigrant communities share their cultures.

People also interact through **immigration**. When people come to live in a new country, they share their culture with the new people they meet. They also learn more about the culture of their new home.

Technology also helps people of different cultures interact. Modern forms of **communication**, such as cell phones and computers, connect people in faraway places. New methods of **transportation** make travel much faster and safer than it used to be.

goods – items that are made and sold

immigration – the act of coming to live in a new country

technology – the use of scientific knowledge to solve problems or make something easier

communication – the exchanging of information

transportation – a way of moving people or goods

By The Way...

Marco Polo took 3 years to travel from Venice to China. Today, people make that trip by airplane in about twelve hours.

KEY IDEA Modern technology helps connect different cultures and nations around the world.

6 *Globalization: Cooperation and Conflict*

What Is Globalization?

The **nations** of the world are becoming more connected. This process is called **globalization**. Globalization is the exchange of cultures, ideas, goods, and **services** around the world.

Marco Polo's travels are an early example of globalization. Today, globalization happens much faster. Technology makes it possible to communicate almost instantly with others. People and goods can move quickly around the world.

Globalization can affect a nation's **economy**. People can visit other countries more easily. The visitors spend money and help the country's economy. When companies open offices in another country, this creates jobs.

▲ This call center in the Philippines helps the customers of a U.S. company. The U.S. company pays for this service.

nations – countries; groups of people living under their own governments

globalization – the exchange of cultures, ideas, goods, and services around the world

services – work, that people do for others

economy – a system of activities related to earning, spending, and managing money

KEY IDEAS
Globalization is the exchange of cultures, ideas, goods, and services around the world. Globalization can affect a nation's economy.

Chapter 1: A World of Cultures

▲ Ecuador earns money by exporting shrimp to other countries.

▲ Ecuador imports computers from the U.S. and other countries.

Globalization and Trade

International **trade** is an important part of globalization. International trade is the exchange of goods and services among nations. In Marco Polo's time, gold and silver were traded for silk, jewels, and spices. Today, nations **export** and **import** a wide range of goods and services.

Nations export, or send, goods and services to other nations. Nations also import, or bring in, goods and services from other nations.

International trade affects a nation's economy. Nations try to export more **products** than they import. When a nation exports products, it earns money. The money can be used to expand businesses and create jobs.

trade – the exchange of goods and services

export – send to another country

import – bring in from another country

products – the goods that a business makes

KEY IDEA International trade is an important part of globalization.

8 *Globalization: Cooperation and Conflict*

YOUR TURN

INTERPRET DATA

China's exports have changed over time. Look at the bar graph. Then answer the questions.

1. Which export increased the most between 1992 and 2005?
2. Which export decreased the most? How much did it decrease?
3. In your own words, explain what the bar graph is showing.

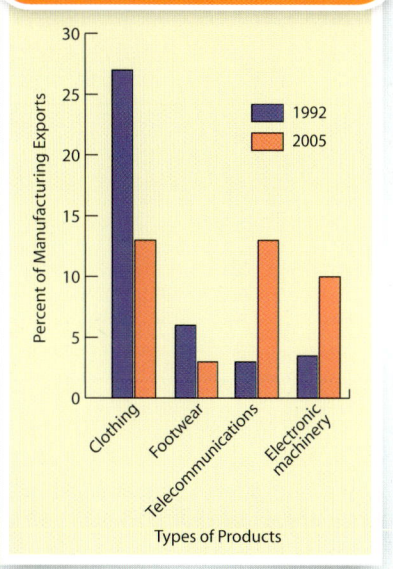

Comparing Some of China's Exports

SOURCE: China Customs, Beijing

MAKE CONNECTIONS

Look at ten items that you use every day. Look for labels that name the countries where the items were made. Mark the countries on a world map. With a group, discuss what these labels show about globalization.

USE THE LANGUAGE OF SOCIAL STUDIES

What is the difference between importing and exporting?

When nations import goods, they bring in goods from other nations. When they export goods, they send goods to other nations.

Chapter 1: A World of Cultures 9

CHAPTER 2

Opportunities and Challenges

Are you a soccer fan? If you want to know the score of a professional soccer game in another country, you can find it on the Internet. This is one of the **benefits**, or helpful effects, of globalization. Globalization has other benefits, too.

Globalization helps companies become more **efficient**. Sometimes a company will save money by making different parts of a product in different countries. For example, an American company might design a video game. Next, artists in the United States, Canada, and Japan draw the art. Computer programmers in India develop the software. Then workers in China put the game on CDs.

benefits – helpful effects
efficient – with the least effort or expense

SHARE IDEAS On a map or a globe, trace the steps in making the video game. How do you think the people in the different countries send their work to each other?

10 *Globalization: Cooperation and Conflict*

In some countries, globalization has created new opportunities. International trade may have increased the number of jobs. This means that more people are able to pay for food, clothing, and shelter. Their children may be able to get a better education.

Better global communication may also has benefits. Doctors from different nations can share information about diseases and medicines. People can learn how other nations are solving problems.

Globalization may offer cultural opportunities as well. When people from different cultures interact, they can learn from each other. They can build cultural understanding. They can enrich their lives with the music, art, and literature of other cultures.

KEY IDEA Globalization can create opportunities for more jobs, better sharing of information, and greater cultural understanding.

▼ The city of Lima, Peru, has grown through globalization.

Chapter 2: Opportunities and Challenges 11

The Challenges of Globalization

Globalization also creates challenges. For example, a company may find that they can pay workers less money in another country. So they move their factories. The company benefits by saving money, but the loss of jobs is a **cost** for the workers.

The loss of jobs can affect an entire community, or even a nation. The people of that community or nation are challenged to create new jobs. Workers may have to be trained for new jobs. Some people may have to move to find new jobs.

costs – losses or sacrifices

These workers are protesting the closing of their factory in the U.S.

As more factories are built, some nations have higher levels of pollution.

Rain forests are being cut down.

Protecting the Environment

The **environment** is another challenge. Some nations do not have strict laws about pollution. The factories in those countries might pollute the air, the water, or the land.

Globalization has also affected the world's rain forests. The rain forests are an important source of the oxygen that we breathe. But many rain forests have been cut down so that the wood can be exported.

As the world economy grows, people use more **fossil fuels**, such as oil and coal, to meet energy needs. But these fuels cause pollution. They are also **nonrenewable**. When they are used up, they cannot be replaced. Nations must face the challenge of finding other sources of energy.

environment – everything in our surroundings; all of nature

fossil fuels – fuels formed millions of years ago from the remains of plants and animals

nonrenewable – cannot be replaced

Chapter 2: Opportunities and Challenges

Protecting Cultures

Globalization can also have a cultural cost. As people from different cultures interact, their cultures may change. One culture may **dominate** other cultures. Cultural beliefs and values may be challenged. People may feel pressure to stop speaking their own languages.

People from different cultures may not understand each other. Instead of getting to know each other, they may form **stereotypes** about each other.

Globalization presents many challenges. But it also creates opportunities for people and nations to work together. People and nations can try to make sure that the benefits of globalization reach more people in the world. They can work together to reduce the costs of globalization.

dominate – have more importance or power

stereotypes – negative ideas about a group of people

Globalization may change traditional ways of life.

Globalization may bring together people from different cultures.

KEY IDEAS The challenges of globalization can include the loss of jobs, environmental problems, and changes in cultural values. Nations can work together to bring the benefits of globalization to more people.

14 *Globalization: Cooperation and Conflict*

YOUR TURN

ANALYZE CAUSE AND EFFECT

Globalization has certain causes and effects. Sometimes a cause has more than one effect. For example, look at the cause/effect flowchart below. What effects could happen in the U.S. and in India? With a partner, discuss the effects of the company's decision.

Cause
A company decides to move its factory from the U.S. to India to save money.

→ What effect does this have in the U.S.?

→ What effect does this have in India?

MAKE CONNECTIONS

Think about the challenges and opportunities of globalization. How has your community been affected by globalization?

 STRATEGY FOCUS

Make Inferences

Make inferences about the photos in this chapter. What do they show about globalization?

Chapter 2: Opportunities and Challenges

CHAPTER 3

Working Together

As global connections increase, more people understand that the nations of the world are **interdependent**. Events in one part of the world affect other parts of the world. Some problems can be solved only if nations work together.

For example, many people are concerned about **climate change**. Scientists are still figuring out how climate change may affect people. But it is already clear that the nations of the world must work together on this issue.

interdependent – dependent, or relying, upon each other

climate change – a long-term change in weather patterns

16 *Globalization: Cooperation and Conflict*

Global **cooperation** will help people face other challenges, too. Providing better education, medical care, and living conditions for all people will require global cooperation.

There are examples of cooperation among the nations of the world. Nations sign trade agreements. Scientists and doctors share information that can help people in different nations.

At the same time, **conflicts** divide some nations of the world. Disagreements about beliefs, resources, and power have led to wars and other forms of violence. Sometimes a history of conflict makes it difficult for nations to find a path to peace.

cooperation – the act of working together
conflicts – disagreements

Explore Language

co- = together, with
cooperate = operate (or work) together

▲ **Nations and people must cooperate to find peaceful ways to resolve conflicts.**

Chapter 3: Working Together 17

Bringing Nations Together

Some international organizations work to end conflict and build cooperation among nations. The United Nations is an important example. There are now 192 member nations. These nations try to end their conflict through discussions and agreements. The United Nations also works on many different projects in different nations. The goals of these projects include promoting peace, providing health care, ending poverty, and protecting the environment.

As nations become more interdependent, organizations like the United Nations become more important. It is also important for people of all cultures to find ways to settle conflict, and to cooperate to make the world a better place.

▼ **International organizations such as the United Nations help nations avoid conflict.**

KEY IDEAS Nations must cooperate in order to end conflict, solve challenges, and promote peace.

Globalization: Cooperation and Conflict

YOUR TURN

READ MAPS

Polio is a disease that is caused by the poliovirus. In 1988, the World Health Organization (WHO) began a campaign to end polio by the year 2000. Use information on the maps to answer these questions.

1. What happened to poliovirus in Africa between 1988 and 2003?
2. WHO did not meet its goal. Do you think the campaign was a success? Share your ideas with a partner.

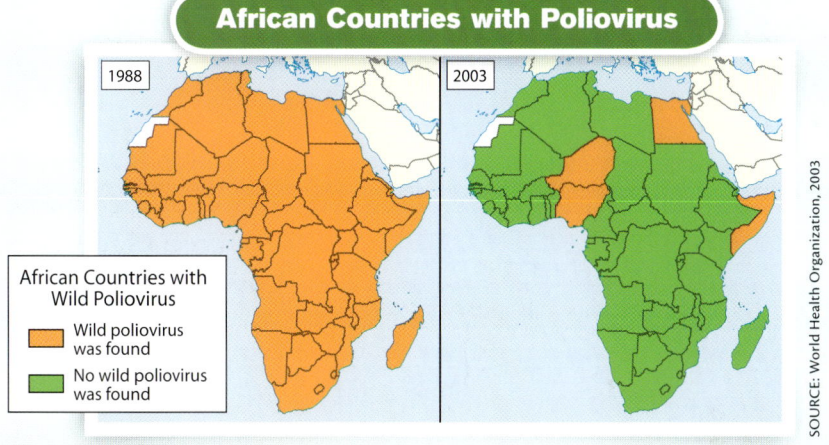

MAKE CONNECTIONS

Think of an organization you know, such as a team or a club. Describe how people in the organization handle conflict and build cooperation.

EXPAND VOCABULARY

The nations of the world are **interdependent**. The prefix *inter-* means "together" or "between." Find out about these words: **interact**, **interfere**, and **intersection**. Explain how each word is related to being together or between things.

Chapter 3: Working Together 19

CAREER EXPLORATIONS

Working for the United Nations

The United Nations (U.N.) is an international organization. It employs more than 14,000 people in jobs around the world.

U.N. workers may be sent to live in other countries. Usually they bring their families. Sometimes the jobs are in dangerous places, so the families stay home.

The chart below gives just a few examples of U.N. careers.

- Find out more about jobs at the United Nations.
- Tell which jobs at the U.N. sound the most interesting to you. Tell why.

Positions	Responsibilities
Interpreter	Attends meetings and translates what people say, for example from Spanish to Russian
Human rights officer	Works on issues such as the rights of children, women's rights, and workers' rights
Video producer	Plans and produces videos about United Nations projects in different countries

▶ United Nations workers help people around the world.

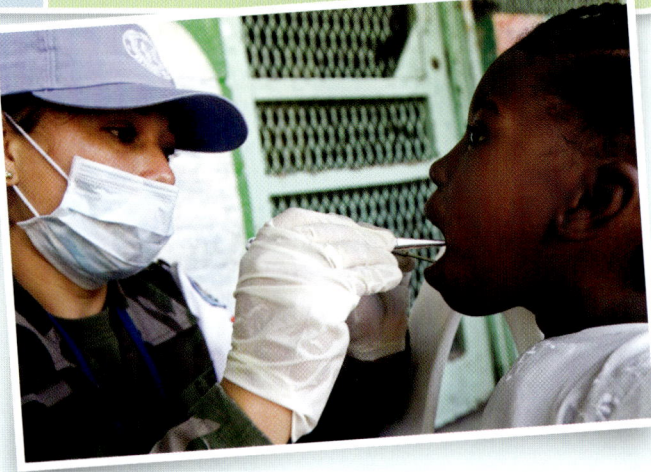

Globalization: Cooperation and Conflict

USE LANGUAGE TO PERSUADE

Words that Persuade

When you feel strongly about something, you want to convince others to feel the same way. You can use words such as **demand**, **must**, and **need**, to help persuade readers to agree with you.

EXAMPLES

Demand action! We **must** work together to give healthcare to people around the world. Millions of people **need** our help.

Talk About It

Look through this book with a partner. Find examples of words that persuade. Discuss what the writer is trying to persuade readers about.

Create a Booklet

Choose one of the challenges of globalization. Create a booklet to persuade people to work on this problem together.

- Describe the challenge.
- Explain what you want people to do to solve the problem.
- Choose words that will help persuade your readers.
- Illustrate your booklet with photos or drawings.

Words You Can Use

Nouns	Adjectives	Verbs
opportunity	dangerous	must
problem	difficult	should
challenge	important	help
solution		

SOCIAL STUDIES AROUND YOU

Water for the World

In some parts of the world, there is a shortage, or lack, of clean drinking water. People have to walk long distances for water, or use water that can make them sick. International organizations are working to provide enough clean drinking water for everyone.

Use the map and the photo to answer these questions.

- In which parts of the world is there a shortage of safe drinking water?

- Locate the United States on the map. What percentage of the population does not have safe drinking water?

- What are some of the challenges people face when they have to walk to get safe drinking water?

Globalization: Cooperation and Conflict

Key Words

communication the exchanging of information
Communication among nations is important for resolving conflicts.

conflict (conflicts) disagreement
International organizations try to resolve conflicts among nations.

cooperation the act of working together for a common purpose
Cooperation among nations can improve trade.

economy (economies) system of activities related to earning, spending, and managing money
New jobs are good for a nation's economy.

environment (environments) everything in our surroundings; all of nature
Nations should work together to protect the environment.

globalization the exchange of cultures, ideas, goods, and services around the world
Marco Polo's travels are an early example of globalization.

interdependent dependent, or relying, upon each other
International trade makes nations interdependent.

nation (nations) a country; a group of people living under their own government
The United States is a nation.

poverty the state of being poor
Global cooperation is needed to reduce poverty around the world.

product (products) a good that a business makes
This company makes paper products.

technology (technologies) the use of scientific knowledge to solve problems or make something easier
Modern technology can make communication easier.

trade the exchange of goods and services
International trade can improve a nation's economy.

transportation a way of moving people or goods
Trains are a form of transportation.

Key Words 23

Index

benefit 14, 15, 16–17
climate change 16
communication 6
conflict 16–18, 19
cooperation 16–18, 19
cost 12–14, 15
culture 4–7, 11, 14, 18
cultural understanding 11
economy 7–8, 9, 12
environment 7–8, 9

export 8, 9, 13, 15
fossil fuels 13
globalization 4–8, 9, 10–14, 15, 16–18, 19, 21
goods 4, 6–8, 9
immigration 6
import 8, 9, 13, 15
interact 5, 6, 11, 14, 19
interdependent 16–18, 19
nation 7–8, 9, 10–14, 15, 16–18, 19, 20

poverty 2–3, 12, 17, 21, 22
product 8, 9, 10
services 7–8, 12, 15
stereotype 14
technology 6–7, 9, 10, 15
trade 4–8, 9, 11, 13, 15
trade agreement 17
transportation 6–7
United Nations 18, 20

MILLMARK EDUCATION CORPORATION
Ericka Markman, President and CEO; Karen Peratt, VP, Editorial Director; Lisa Bingen, VP, Marketing; Dave Willette, VP, Sales; Rachel L. Moir, VP, Operations and Production; Shelby Alinsky, Associate Editor; Janet Battiste, Language Editor; Pictures Unlimited, Photo Research; Arleen Nakama, Technology Projects

PROGRAM AUTHORS
Mary Hawley, Program Author, Instructional Design
Peggy Altoff, Program Author, Social Studies

STUDENT BOOK DEVELOPMENT
Gare Thompson Associates, Inc.

BOOK DESIGN
Dinardo Design LLC

TECHNOLOGY
Six Red Marbles

CONTENT REVIEWER
Margit McGuire, PhD, Program Director and Professor of Teacher Education, Seattle University, Seattle, WA

PROGRAM ADVISORS
Scott K. Baker, PhD, Pacific Institutes for Research, Eugene, OR
Carla C. Johnson, EdD, University of Toledo, Toledo, OH
Margit McGuire, PhD, Seattle University, Seattle, WA
Donna Ogle, EdD, National-Louis University, Chicago, IL
Betty Ansin Smallwood, PhD, Center for Applied Linguistics, Washington, DC
Gail Thompson, PhD, Claremont Graduate University, Claremont, CA
Emma Violand-Sánchez, EdD, Arlington Public Schools, Arlington, VA (retired)

PHOTO CREDITS Cover ©Dominique Derda/France 2/Corbis; IFC and 15b ©David Safanda/iStockphoto.com; 1a ©Rob Wilson/Shutterstock; 2a, 4a, 7a, 8b, 9a, 19a, 22a Mapping Specialists; 2-3a David H. Wells/Getty Images; 3a ©AP Photo/Shakil Adil; 3b Wally Nell/ZUMA Press; 4b ©The Print Collector/age fotostock; 5a ©Hulton Archive/Getty Images; 5b ©The Bridgeman Art Library; 6a ©Gail Mooney/CORBIS; 6b ©Mint Photography/Alamy; 7b ©AFP/Getty Images; 8a ©Dpto. Revista Aqua Cultura, Guayaquil, Ecuador; 8c ©ene/Shutterstock; 9b and 9c Photos by Ken Karp; 10a ©David Young-Wolff/Photo Edit; 10b ©Ronald Sumners/Shutterstock; 11a and 24a ©José Fuste Raga/age fotostock; 12a ©AP Images/Jocelyn Williams; 13a ©Jon Bower/age fotostock; 13b ©Josè Enrique Molina/age fotostock; 14a ©Jim West/Alamy; 14b ©Peter Johnson/CORBIS; 16a ©AP Images/Jacques Boissinot; 17a ©AP Images/The Press Democrat; 18a ©AP Images/Richard Drew; 20a ©UN Photo Library; 22b ©Factoria Singular/age fotostock; 23a ©David H. Wells/Getty Images

Copyright ©2009 Millmark Education Corporation

All rights reserved. Reproduction of the whole or any part of the contents without written permission from the publisher is prohibited. Millmark Education and ConceptLinks are registered trademarks of Millmark Education Corporation.

Published by Millmark Education Corporation
PO Box 30824
Bethesda, MD 20824

ISBN-13: 978-1-4334-0675-1

Printed in the USA

10 9 8 7 6 5 4 3 2 1

24 *Globalization: Cooperation and Conflict*